JOY & RADIANCE

In the Words of 'Abdu'l-Bahá

Bahá'í Publishing
401 Greenleaf Avenue, Wilmette, Illinois 60091

Printed in the United States of America on acid-free paper ∞
24 23 22 21 4 3 2 1

ISBN 978-1-61851-201-7

Cover design by Carlos Esparza
Book design by Patrick Falso

Extract 16 is from *The Secret of Divine Civilization*. Wilmette, IL: Bahá'í Publishing, 2007.

Extracts 19, 21, 28 are from *Selections from the Writings of 'Abdu'l-Bahá*. Wilmette, IL: Bahá'í Publishing, 2010.

Extract 20 is from *Some Answered Questions*. Haifa: Bahá'í World Centre, 2014.

Extract 8 is from *'Abdu'l-Bahá in London: Addresses and Notes of Conversations*. London: Bahá'í Publishing Trust, 1982.

Extracts 1, 2, 5, 10, 15 are from *Paris Talks: Addresses Given by 'Abdu'l-Bahá in Paris in 1911*. Wilmette, IL: Bahá'í Publishing, 2011.

Extracts 3, 4, 6, 7, 9, 11–14, 17, 18, 22–27 are from *The Promulgation of Universal Peace: Talks Delivered by 'Abdu'l-Bahá during His Visit to the United States and Canada in 1912*. Wilmette, IL: Bahá'í Publishing, 2012.

‘Abdu’l-Bahá

November 2021 will mark the hundredth anniversary of the passing of a figure beloved by many. ‘Abdu’l-Bahá, meaning *Servant of the Glory,* is the title assumed by Abbás Effendi (1844–1921), the son and appointed successor of Bahá’u’lláh—the Prophet and Founder of the Bahá’í Faith. ‘Abdu’l-Bahá shared a lifetime of exile with his Father at the hands of the Persian and Ottoman Empires, and was a prisoner for forty years. Despite the severe hardships that characterized his life, he dedicated his energy to the service of others and radiated joy and selfless contentment at all times. His charitable deeds and undiscriminating love for all are well documented in the accounts of countless souls who crossed his path, and his timeless and deep wisdom is recorded extensively in both his written works and in the transcripts of his many public addresses. He is known by Bahá’ís as the perfect exemplar of the Faith’s teachings.

1

In this world we are influenced by two sentiments, *Joy* and *Pain.*

Joy gives us wings! In times of joy our strength is more vital, our intellect keener, and our understanding less clouded. We seem better able to cope with the world and to find our sphere of usefulness. But when sadness visits us we become weak, our strength leaves us, our comprehension is dim and our intelligence veiled. The actualities of life seem to elude our grasp, the eyes of our spirits fail to discover the sacred mysteries, and we become even as dead beings.

There is no human being untouched by these two influences; but all the sorrow and the grief that exist come from the world of matter—the spiritual world bestows only the joy!

2

I myself was in prison forty years—one year alone would have been impossible to bear—nobody survived that imprisonment more than a year! But, thank God, during all those forty years I was supremely happy! Every day, on waking, it was like hearing good tidings, and every night infinite joy was mine. Spirituality was my comfort, and turning to God was my greatest joy. If this had not been so, do you think it possible that I could have lived through those forty years in prison?

Thus, spirituality is the greatest of God's gifts. . . .

3

Turn all your thoughts toward bringing joy to hearts. Beware! Beware! lest ye offend any heart. Assist the world of humanity as much as possible. Be the source of consolation to every sad one, assist every weak one, be helpful to every indigent one, care for every sick one, be the cause of glorification to every lowly one, and shelter those who are overshadowed by fear.

4

The first sign of faith is love. The message of the holy, divine Manifestations is love; the phenomena of creation are based upon love; the radiance of the world is due to love; the well-being and happiness of the world depend upon it. Therefore, I admonish you that you must strive throughout the human world to diffuse the light of love.

5

If your days on earth are numbered, you know that everlasting life awaits you. If material anxiety envelops you in a dark cloud, spiritual radiance lightens your path. Verily, those whose minds are illumined by the Spirit of the Most High have supreme consolation.

6

When the mists and darkness of superstition and prejudice are dispersed, all will see the Sun aright and alike. Then will all nations become as one in its radiance.

Inasmuch as these clouds and human vapors of superstition hide the light of the spiritual Sun, we must put forth our utmost endeavor to dispel them. May we unite in this and be enlightened to accomplish it, for the Sun is one and its radiance and bounty universal. All the inhabitants of earth are recipients of the bounty of the one phenomenal sun, and none are preferred above others; so, likewise, all receive the heavenly bestowals of the Word of God; none are specialized as favorites; all are under its protection and universal effulgence.

7

There are lamps which illumine small places and lamps which illumine the horizons. The lamp of the guidance of God, wherever lighted, has shed its radiance throughout the East and the West. Praise be to God!

8

One who is imprisoned by desires is always unhappy; the children of the Kingdom have unchained themselves from their desires. Break all fetters and seek for spiritual joy and enlightenment; then, though you walk on this earth, you will perceive yourselves to be within the divine horizon.

9

Material progress ensures the happiness of the human world. Spiritual progress ensures the happiness and eternal continuance of the soul.

10

. . . the trials which beset our every step, all our sorrow, pain, shame and grief, are born in the world of matter; whereas the spiritual Kingdom never causes sadness. A man living with his thoughts in this Kingdom knows perpetual joy. The ills all flesh is heir to do not pass him by, but they only touch the surface of his life, the depths are calm and serene.

11

For just as the night, when it becomes excessively dark, precedes the dawn of a new day, so likewise when the darkness of religious apathy and heedlessness overtakes the world, when human souls become negligent of God, when materialistic ideas overshadow spirituality, when nations become submerged in the world of matter and forget God—at such a time as this shall the divine Sun shine forth and the radiant morn appear.

12

The Blessed Perfection, Bahá'u'lláh, endured hardships and vicissitudes nearly fifty years. There was no ordeal or difficulty He did not experience, yet He endured all in perfect joy and happiness.

Those who beheld Him were assured of His great happiness, for no trace of sadness or sorrow was ever visible upon His face. Even in prison He was like a king enthroned in majesty and greatness, and He ever bore Himself with supreme confidence and dignity.

13

Observe how rarely human souls sacrifice their pleasure or comfort for others. . . . Yet all the divine Manifestations suffered, offered Their lives and blood, sacrificed Their existence, comfort and all They possessed for the sake of mankind. Therefore, consider how much They love. Were it not for Their love for humanity, spiritual love would be mere nomenclature. Were it not for Their illumination, human souls would not be radiant. How effective is Their love! This is a sign of the love of God, a ray of the Sun of Reality.

14

. . . be ye rejoiced, for ye are sheltered beneath the providence of God. Be happy and joyous because the bestowals of God are intended for you and the life of the Holy Spirit is breathing upon you.

Rejoice, for the heavenly table is prepared for you.

Rejoice, for the angels of heaven are your assistants and helpers.

Rejoice, for the glance of the Blessed Beauty, Bahá'u'lláh, is directed upon you.

Rejoice, for Bahá'u'lláh is your Protector.

Rejoice, for the everlasting glory is destined for you.

Rejoice, for the eternal life is awaiting you.

15

If the heart turns away from the blessings God offers how can it hope for happiness? If it does not put its hope and trust in God's Mercy, where can it find rest? Oh, trust in God! for His Bounty is everlasting, and in His Blessings, for they are superb. Oh! put your faith in the Almighty, for He faileth not and His goodness endureth for ever! His Sun giveth Light continually, and the Clouds of His Mercy are full of the Waters of Compassion with which He waters the hearts of all who trust in Him. His refreshing Breeze ever carries healing in its wings to the parched souls of men!

16

. . . the happiness and greatness, the rank and station, the pleasure and peace, of an individual have never consisted in his personal wealth, but rather in his excellent character, his high resolve, the breadth of his learning, and his ability to solve difficult problems.

17

Your utmost desire must be to confer happiness upon each other. Each one must be the servant of the others, thoughtful of their comfort and welfare. In the path of God one must forget himself entirely. He must not consider his own pleasure but seek the pleasure of others. He must not desire glory nor gifts of bounty for himself but seek these gifts and blessings for his brothers and sisters.

18

May the world of humanity find peace and composure and this dark earth be transformed into a realm of radiance. May the East and West clasp hands together. May the oneness of God become reflected and fully revealed in the hearts of humanity and all mankind prove to be the manifestations of the favors of God.

19

Let all your striving be for this, to become the source of life and immortality, and peace and comfort and joy, to every human soul, whether one known to you or a stranger, one opposed to you or on your side.

20

The reality of the Divinity is even as the sun, which from the heights of its sanctity shines upon every land, and of whose radiance every land and every soul receives a share. Were it not for this light and this radiance, nothing could exist.

21

In this day, to thank God for His bounties consisteth in possessing a radiant heart, and a soul open to the promptings of the spirit. This is the essence of thanksgiving.

22

The world of humanity is filled with darkness; you are its radiant candles. It is very poor; you must be the treasury of the Kingdom. It is exceedingly debased; you must be the cause of its exaltation. It is bereft of divine graces; you must give it impetus and spiritual quickening. According to the teachings of Bahá'u'lláh you must love and cherish each individual member of humanity.

23

Let your hearts be as mirrors in which the radiance of the Sun of Reality is visible.

24

. . . the honor of the human kingdom is the attainment of spiritual happiness in the human world, the acquisition of the knowledge and love of God. The honor allotted to man is the acquisition of the supreme virtues of the human world. This is his real happiness and felicity. But if material happiness and spiritual felicity be conjoined, it will be "delight upon delight."

25

I desire to make manifest among the friends in America a new light that they may become a new people, that a new foundation may be established and complete harmony be realized; for the foundation of Bahá'u'lláh is love. . . . You must have infinite love for each other, each preferring the other before himself. The people must be so attracted to you that they will exclaim, "What happiness exists among you!" and will see in your faces the lights of the Kingdom; then in wonderment they will turn to you and seek the cause of your happiness. You must give the message through action and deed, not alone by word. Word must be conjoined with deed. You must love your friend better than yourself; yes, be willing to sacrifice yourself. . . . I want you to be happy . . . to laugh, smile and rejoice in order that others may be made happy by you.

26

In this great Cause the light of guidance is shining and radiant. Bahá'u'lláh has even said that occupation and labor are devotion. All humanity must obtain a livelihood by sweat of the brow and bodily exertion, at the same time seeking to lift the burden of others, striving to be the source of comfort to souls and facilitating the means of living. This in itself is devotion to God.

27

Consider how great has been the progress in this radiant century. Civilization has unfolded. Nations have developed. Industrialism and jurisprudence have expanded. Sciences, inventions and discoveries have increased. All of these show that the world of existence is continuously progressing and developing; and therefore, assuredly, the virtues characterizing the maturity of man must, likewise, expand and grow.

28

If only thou couldst know what a high station is destined for those souls who are severed from the world, are powerfully attracted to the Faith, and are teaching, under the sheltering shadow of Bahá'u'lláh! How thou wouldst rejoice, how thou wouldst, in exultation and rapture, spread thy wings and soar heavenward—for being a follower of such a way, and a traveler toward such a Kingdom.